READING NOTEBOOK & JOURNAL

FOR ADULT STUDENTS

BY COACHING FOR BETTER LEARNING

"Today a reader, tomorrow a leader."

– Margaret Fuller

This Reading Notebook & Journal is designed to help adult learners to take good notes, reflect on their reading performance, and plan their practice/reading time.

Name: ____

Lesson: ______________________ **Date:** __________ **Time:** ________

Objectives: ____

Notes or Strategies

New words or Phrases

Lesson or Passage Summary

Reading strategies that I learned.

New words or phrases I leaned.

Questions that I have.

1. ______
2. ______
3. ______
4. ______
5. ______

What I need to reread or review.

What I need help with.

What I will prepare for next class (Assignment)

Questions for next class.

My target practice/reading time: ______________________

Reward for meeting my reading target: ______________________

What I will do better in the next time.

General Notes

Lesson: ______________________________ **Date:** __________ **Time:** ________

Objectives: ____

Notes or Strategies

New words or Phrases

Lesson or Passage Summary

Reading strategies that I learned.	New words or phrases I leaned.

Questions that I have.

1.
2.
3.
4.
5.

What I need to reread or review.

What I need help with.

What I will prepare for next class (Assignment)

Questions for next class.

My target practice/reading time:

Reward for meeting my reading target:

What I will do better in the next time.

General Notes

Lesson: ______________________ **Date:** __________ **Time:** ________

Objectives: ____

Notes or Strategies

New words or Phrases

Lesson or Passage Summary

Reading strategies that I learned.

New words or phrases I leaned.

Questions that I have.

1. __________
2. __________
3. __________
4. __________
5. __________

What I need to reread or review.

What I need help with.

What I will prepare for next class (Assignment)

	Questions for next class.

My target practice/reading time: ____________________

Reward for meeting my reading target: ____________________

What I will do better in the next time.

General Notes

Lesson: ______________________ **Date:** __________ **Time:** ________

Objectives: ____

Notes or Strategies

New words or Phrases

Lesson or Passage Summary

Reading strategies that I learned.

New words or phrases I leaned.

Questions that I have.

1.

2.

3.

4.

5.

What I need to reread or review.

What I need help with.

What I will prepare for next class (Assignment)

Questions for next class.

My target practice/reading time: ________________

Reward for meeting my reading target: ________________

What I will do better in the next time.

General Notes

Lesson: ______________________ Date: __________ Time: ________

Objectives: ____

Notes or Strategies

New words or Phrases

Lesson or Passage Summary

Reading strategies that I learned.	New words or phrases I leaned.

Questions that I have.

1. ___
2. ___
3. ___
4. ___
5. ___

What I need to reread or review.

What I need help with.

What I will prepare for next class (Assignment)

	Questions for next class.

My target practice/reading time: ______________________

Reward for meeting my reading target: ______________________

What I will do better in the next time.

General Notes

Lesson: ______________________________ Date: __________ Time: ________

Objectives: ____

Notes or Strategies

New words or Phrases

Lesson or Passage Summary

Reading strategies that I learned.

New words or phrases I leaned.

Questions that I have.

1. ______________________________
2. ______________________________
3. ______________________________
4. ______________________________
5. ______________________________

What I need to reread or review.

What I need help with.

What I will prepare for next class (Assignment)

	Questions for next class.

My target practice/reading time: ______________________

Reward for meeting my reading target: ______________________

What I will do better in the next time.

General Notes

Lesson: ______________________ **Date:** __________ **Time:** ________

Objectives: ____

Notes or Strategies

New words or Phrases

Lesson or Passage Summary

Reading strategies that I learned.	New words or phrases I leaned.

Questions that I have.

1.
2.
3.
4.
5.

What I need to reread or review.

What I need help with.

What I will prepare for next class (Assignment)

	Questions for next class.

My target practice/reading time: ______________________

Reward for meeting my reading target: ______________________

What I will do better in the next time.

General Notes

Lesson: ______________________ **Date:** __________ **Time:** ________

Objectives: ____

Notes or Strategies

New words or Phrases

Lesson or Passage Summary

Reading strategies that I learned.	New words or phrases I leaned.

Questions that I have.

1. ______
2. ______
3. ______
4. ______
5. ______

What I need to reread or review.

What I need help with.

What I will prepare for next class (Assignment)

	Questions for next class.

My target practice/reading time: ________________

Reward for meeting my reading target: ________________

What I will do better in the next time.

General Notes

Lesson: ______________________________ **Date:** __________ **Time:** ________

Objectives: ____

Notes or Strategies

New words or Phrases

Lesson or Passage Summary

Reading strategies that I learned.	New words or phrases I leaned.

Questions that I have.

1.
2.
3.
4.
5.

What I need to reread or review.

What I need help with.

What I will prepare for next class (Assignment)

	Questions for next class.

My target practice/reading time: ____________________

Reward for meeting my reading target: ____________________

What I will do better in the next time.

General Notes

Lesson: ______________________ **Date:** __________ **Time:** ________

Objectives: ____

Notes or Strategies

New words or Phrases

Lesson or Passage Summary

Reading strategies that I learned.

New words or phrases I leaned.

Questions that I have.

1. ____________________
2. ____________________
3. ____________________
4. ____________________
5. ____________________

What I need to reread or review.

What I need help with.

What I will prepare for next class (Assignment)

	Questions for next class.

My target practice/reading time: ____________

Reward for meeting my reading target: ____________

What I will do better in the next time.

General Notes

Lesson: ______________________________ **Date:** __________ **Time:** ________

Objectives: ____

Notes or Strategies

New words or Phrases

Lesson or Passage Summary

Reading strategies that I learned.

New words or phrases I leaned.

Questions that I have.

1.
2.
3.
4.
5.

What I need to reread or review.

What I need help with.

What I will prepare for next class (Assignment)

	Questions for next class.

My target practice/reading time: ______________________

Reward for meeting my reading target: ______________________

What I will do better in the next time.

General Notes

Lesson: ______________________________ **Date:** __________ **Time:** ________

Objectives: ____

Notes or Strategies

New words or Phrases

Lesson or Passage Summary

Reading strategies that I learned.	New words or phrases I leaned.

Questions that I have.

1. ________________
2. ________________
3. ________________
4. ________________
5. ________________

What I need to reread or review.

What I need help with.

What I will prepare for next class (Assignment)

Questions for next class.

My target practice/reading time:

Reward for meeting my reading target:

What I will do better in the next time.

General Notes

Lesson: ______________________ **Date:** __________ **Time:** ________

Objectives: ____

Notes or Strategies

New words or Phrases

Lesson or Passage Summary

Reading strategies that I learned.	New words or phrases I leaned.

Questions that I have.

1. ________________
2. ________________
3. ________________
4. ________________
5. ________________

What I need to reread or review.

What I need help with.

What I will prepare for next class (Assignment)

	Questions for next class.

My target practice/reading time: ____________________

Reward for meeting my reading target: ____________________

What I will do better in the next time.

General Notes

Lesson: ______________________________ Date: __________ Time: ________

Objectives: ____

Notes or Strategies

New words or Phrases

Lesson or Passage Summary

Reading strategies that I learned.

New words or phrases I leaned.

Questions that I have.

1. ______
2. ______
3. ______
4. ______
5. ______

What I need to reread or review.

What I need help with.

What I will prepare for next class (Assignment)

	Questions for next class.

My target practice/reading time: ______________________

Reward for meeting my reading target: ______________________

What I will do better in the next time.

General Notes

Lesson: ______________________________ Date: __________ Time: ________

Objectives: ____

Notes or Strategies

New words or Phrases

Lesson or Passage Summary

Reading strategies that I learned.

New words or phrases I leaned.

Questions that I have.

1. ____________________

2. ____________________

3. ____________________

4. ____________________

5. ____________________

What I need to reread or review.

What I need help with.

What I will prepare for next class (Assignment)

Questions for next class.

My target practice/reading time:

Reward for meeting my reading target:

What I will do better in the next time.

General Notes

Lesson: ______________________ **Date:** __________ **Time:** ________

Objectives: ____

Notes or Strategies

New words or Phrases

Lesson or Passage Summary

Reading strategies that I learned.

New words or phrases I leaned.

Questions that I have.

1. ______
2. ______
3. ______
4. ______
5. ______

What I need to reread or review.

What I need help with.

What I will prepare for next class (Assignment)

	Questions for next class.

My target practice/reading time: ______________________

Reward for meeting my reading target: ______________________

What I will do better in the next time.

General Notes

Lesson: ______________________ **Date:** __________ **Time:** __________

Objectives: ____

Notes or Strategies

New words or Phrases

Lesson or Passage Summary

Reading strategies that I learned.

New words or phrases I leaned.

Questions that I have.

1. ______
2. ______
3. ______
4. ______
5. ______

What I need to reread or review.

What I need help with.

What I will prepare for next class (Assignment)

	Questions for next class.

My target practice/reading time: ________________

Reward for meeting my reading target: ________________

What I will do better in the next time.

General Notes

Lesson: ______________________________ **Date:** __________ **Time:** ________

Objectives: ____

Notes or Strategies

New words or Phrases

Lesson or Passage Summary

Reading strategies that I learned.

New words or phrases I leaned.

Questions that I have.

1. ___
2. ___
3. ___
4. ___
5. ___

What I need to reread or review.

What I need help with.

What I will prepare for next class (Assignment)

Questions for next class.

My target practice/reading time:

Reward for meeting my reading target:

What I will do better in the next time.

General Notes

Lesson: ______________________________ Date: __________ Time: ________

Objectives: ____

Notes or Strategies

New words or Phrases

Lesson or Passage Summary

Reading strategies that I learned.

New words or phrases I leaned.

Questions that I have.

1.
2.
3.
4.
5.

What I need to reread or review.

What I need help with.

What I will prepare for next class (Assignment)

	Questions for next class.

My target practice/reading time: ______________________

Reward for meeting my reading target: ______________________

What I will do better in the next time.

General Notes

Lesson: ______________________ Date: __________ Time: ________

Objectives: ____

Notes or Strategies

New words or Phrases

Lesson or Passage Summary

Reading strategies that I learned.

New words or phrases I leaned.

Questions that I have.

1. ___
2. ___
3. ___
4. ___
5. ___

What I need to reread or review.

What I need help with.

What I will prepare for next class (Assignment)

	Questions for next class.

My target practice/reading time: ______________________

Reward for meeting my reading target: ______________________

What I will do better in the next time.

General Notes

Lesson: ______________________________ **Date:** __________ **Time:** ________

Objectives: ____

Notes or Strategies

New words or Phrases

Lesson or Passage Summary

Reading strategies that I learned.

New words or phrases I leaned.

Questions that I have.

1.
2.
3.
4.
5.

What I need to reread or review.

What I need help with.

What I will prepare for next class (Assignment)

	Questions for next class.

My target practice/reading time: __________

Reward for meeting my reading target: __________

What I will do better in the next time.

General Notes

Lesson: ______________________________ **Date:** __________ **Time:** ________

Objectives: ____

Notes or Strategies

New words or Phrases

Lesson or Passage Summary

Reading strategies that I learned.

New words or phrases I leaned.

Questions that I have.

1. ____
2. ____
3. ____
4. ____
5. ____

What I need to reread or review.

What I need help with.

What I will prepare for next class (Assignment)

Questions for next class.

My target practice/reading time: ______________________

Reward for meeting my reading target: ______________________

What I will do better in the next time.

General Notes

Lesson: ______________________ **Date:** __________ **Time:** ________

Objectives: ____

Notes or Strategies

New words or Phrases

Lesson or Passage Summary

Reading strategies that I learned.

New words or phrases I leaned.

Questions that I have.

1. ___
2. ___
3. ___
4. ___
5. ___

What I need to reread or review.

What I need help with.

What I will prepare for next class (Assignment)

Questions for next class.

My target practice/reading time: ______________________

Reward for meeting my reading target: ______________________

What I will do better in the next time.

General Notes

2022

July

S	M	T	W	T	F	S
					1	2
3	4	5	6	7	8	9
10	11	12	13	14	15	16
17	18	19	20	21	22	23
24	25	26	27	28	29	30
31						

August

S	M	T	W	T	F	S
	1	2	3	4	5	6
7	8	9	10	11	12	13
14	15	16	17	18	19	20
21	22	23	24	25	26	27
28	29	30	31			

September

S	M	T	W	T	F	S
				1	2	3
4	5	6	7	8	9	10
11	12	13	14	15	16	17
18	19	20	21	22	23	24
25	26	27	28	29	30	

October

S	M	T	W	T	F	S
						1
2	3	4	5	6	7	8
9	10	11	12	13	14	15
16	17	18	19	20	21	22
23	24	25	26	27	28	29
30	31					

November

S	M	T	W	T	F	S
		1	2	3	4	5
6	7	8	9	10	11	12
13	14	15	16	17	18	19
20	21	22	23	24	25	26
27	28	29	30			

December

S	M	T	W	T	F	S
				1	2	3
4	5	6	7	8	9	10
11	12	13	14	15	16	17
18	19	20	21	22	23	24
25	26	27	28	29	30	31

Notes

2023

January

S	M	T	W	T	F	S
1	2	3	4	5	6	7
8	9	10	11	12	13	14
15	16	17	18	19	20	21
22	23	24	25	26	27	28
29	30	31				

February

S	M	T	W	T	F	S
			1	2	3	4
5	6	7	8	9	10	11
12	13	14	15	16	17	18
19	20	21	22	23	24	25
26	27	28				

March

S	M	T	W	T	F	S
			1	2	3	4
5	6	7	8	9	10	11
12	13	14	15	16	17	18
19	20	21	22	23	24	25
26	27	28	29	30	31	

April

S	M	T	W	T	F	S
						1
2	3	4	5	6	7	8
9	10	11	12	13	14	15
16	17	18	19	20	21	22
23	24	25	26	27	28	29
30						

May

S	M	T	W	T	F	S
	1	2	3	4	5	6
7	8	9	10	11	12	13
14	15	16	17	18	19	20
21	22	23	24	25	26	27
28	29	30	31			

June

S	M	T	W	T	F	S
				1	2	3
4	5	6	7	8	9	10
11	12	13	14	15	16	17
18	19	20	21	22	23	24
25	26	27	28	29	30	

July

S	M	T	W	T	F	S
						1
2	3	4	5	6	7	8
9	10	11	12	13	14	15
16	17	18	19	20	21	22
23	24	25	26	27	28	29
30	31					

August

S	M	T	W	T	F	S
		1	2	3	4	5
6	7	8	9	10	11	12
13	14	15	16	17	18	19
20	21	22	23	24	25	26
27	28	29	30	31		

September

S	M	T	W	T	F	S
					1	2
3	4	5	6	7	8	9
10	11	12	13	14	15	16
17	18	19	20	21	22	23
24	25	26	27	28	29	30

October

S	M	T	W	T	F	S
1	2	3	4	5	6	7
8	9	10	11	12	13	14
15	16	17	18	19	20	21
22	23	24	25	26	27	28
29	30	31				

November

S	M	T	W	T	F	S
			1	2	3	4
5	6	7	8	9	10	11
12	13	14	15	16	17	18
19	20	21	22	23	24	25
26	27	28	29	30		

December

S	M	T	W	T	F	S
					1	2
3	4	5	6	7	8	9
10	11	12	13	14	15	16
17	18	19	20	21	22	23
24	25	26	27	28	29	30
31						

READING LOG

NO.	BOOK TITLE	START - END DATE	NO. OF PAGES
1			
2			
3			
4			
5			
6			
7			
8			
9			
10			
11			
12			
13			
14			
15			
16			
17			
18			
19			
20			

READING LOG

NO.	BOOK TITLE	START - END DATE	NO. OF PAGES
21			
22			
23			
24			
25			
26			
27			
28			
29			
30			
31			
32			
33			
34			
35			
36			
37			
38			
39			
40			

About Coaching For Better Learning

We promote systematic solutions, innovative ideas, and future-oriented strategies in adult education, workforce development, and vocational training.

We help build systems to lead adult students closer to their dreams.

Send questions or suggestions to teamcbl@coachingforbetterlearning.com.

By the same publisher:

Student textbooks that save instructors time and promote reflective learning to keep learners engaged.

adulteducationhub.com

Website: https://adulteducationhub.com/